bite size
truth

bite size
truth

meditations for life
book 2

Xin-Rain

BALBOA.
PRESS

A DIVISION OF HAY HOUSE

Balboa Press books may be ordered through booksellers or by contacting:

Balboa Press
A Division of Hay House
1663 Liberty Drive
Bloomington, IN 47403
www.balboapress.com
1 (877) 407-4847

Print information available on the last page.

ISBN: 978-1-5043-3865-3 (sc)
ISBN: 978-1-5043-3866-0 (e)

Balboa Press rev. date: 01/06/2016

Creator once said to Tuka,

"Even I am ever changing—
I am ever beyond
Myself,

What I may have once put my seal upon,
may no longer be
the greatest
Truth."

Tukaram (c. 1608-1649)

as

one

about

two

we

muse

2

(un)name

it;

walk

light

through

it

make-shift,

remembrance;

of

solar-center;

of

roaring-thunder

awe

struck

intent;

to

reason's

bafflement

within

water

water

within;

natural

origin

invisibly

inked;

this

that;

not

distinct

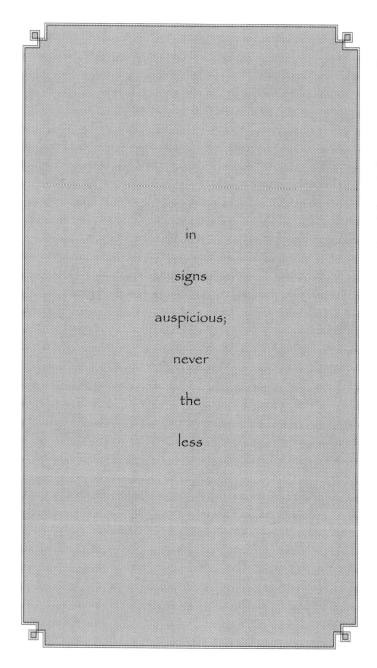

in

signs

auspicious;

never

the

less

ultimate

manifest

wish;

it

already

is

helix-inspired;

nature's

wanderings;

ecstatic

emphatic

not-doing

as

sacred

mandala;

ocean

wave,

swallows

resonating

oneness;

all

that

one

does

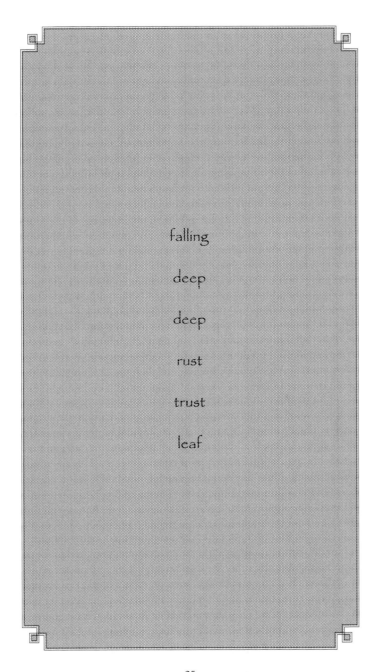

falling

deep

deep

rust

trust

leaf

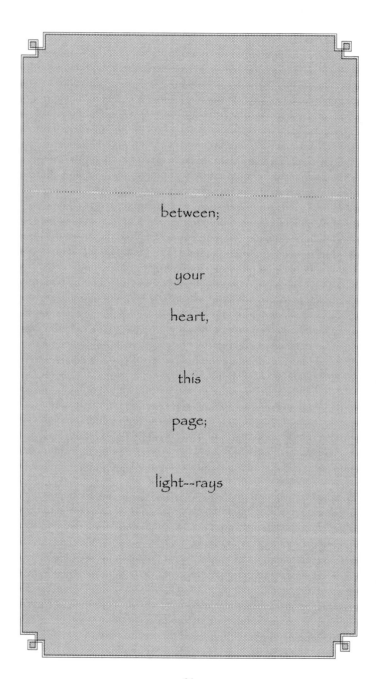

between;

your

heart,

this

page;

light--rays

sun

drenched

stone

dragon

fly

home

nuance;

of

circumstance;

of

unforeseen;

balance

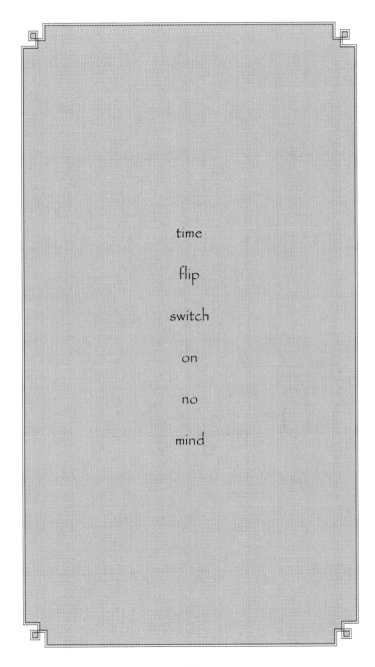

time

flip

switch

on

no

mind

path,

way;

middle

gate;

remain,

remain

adroit

adept

abundant;

empty

form-free

oneness

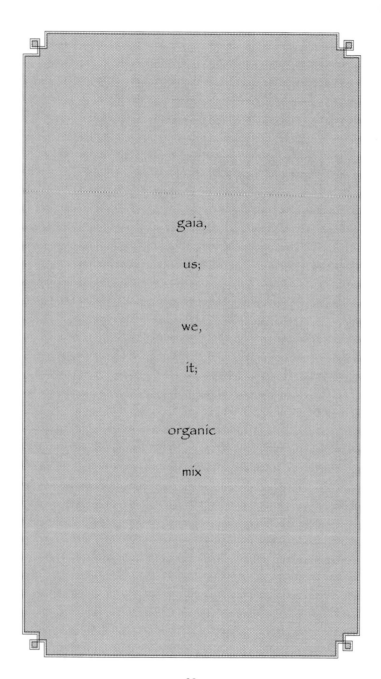

gaia,

us;

we,

it;

organic

mix

baby

duck

swim

cosmos

essence

within

perception

shape

shifts

precisely

what

is

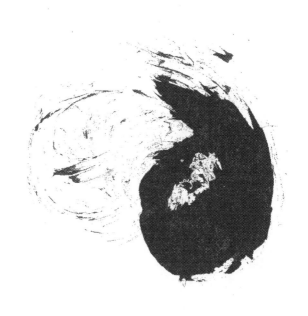

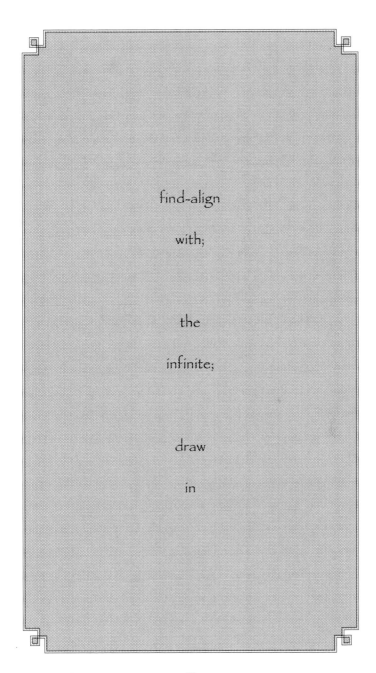

find-align

with;

the

infinite;

draw

in

nature's

heart

strings

strum

eco

system

such

grand

mother

love

other

worldly

(in)flux

alas;

detour

as/is

same

path

is

not

earth

dance

common

opulence

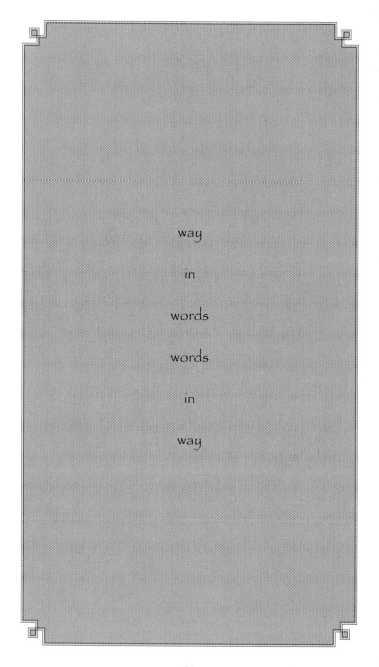

way

in

words

words

in

way

mindfulness;

now-one

quakes

awake;

impermanence,

embrace

tree

trunk

leaves

up

love

drunk

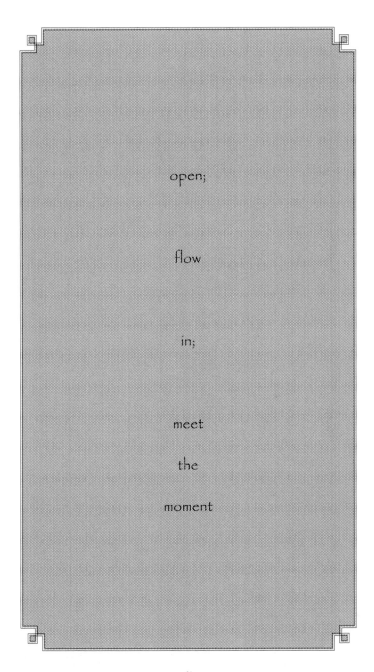

open;

flow

in;

meet

the

moment

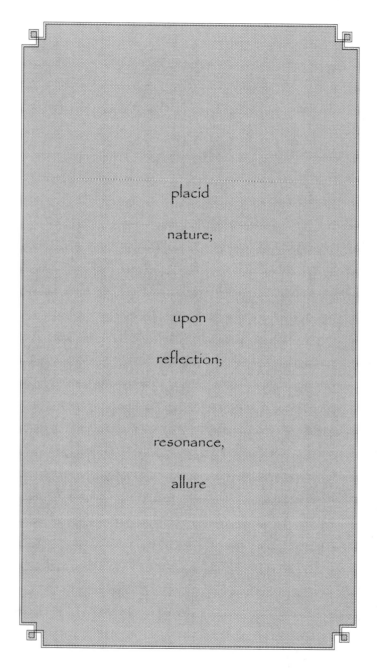

placid

nature;

upon

reflection;

resonance,

allure

what

is;

note

this;

a

practice

midnight

moon;

bid

adieu;

shone,

through

void

to

block;

carve

circle

back

blue

bird

blue

sky

tongue

tide

undone

task

rhapsody;

already

past

capacity

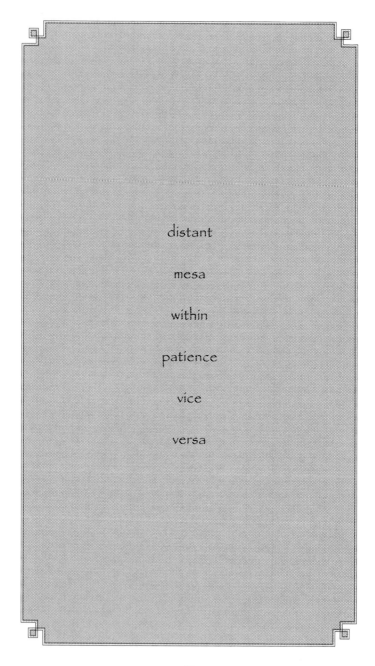

distant

mesa

within

patience

vice

versa

all,

as

sage;

smoke

swirls

play

one's

boundless

jurisdiction;

hidden,

in

intermittence

sea

now

what

one

once

saw

in

to

it;

intuit

intuit

intuit

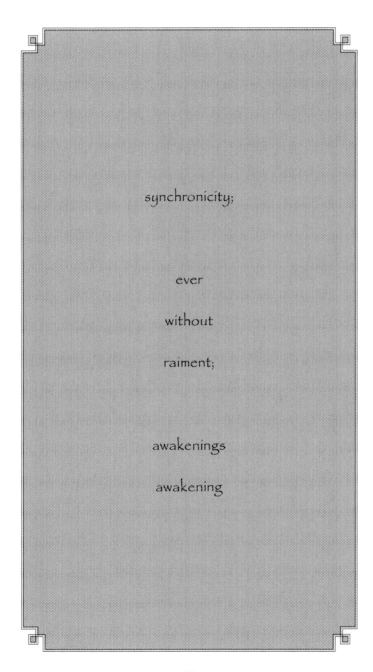

synchronicity;

ever

without

raiment;

awakenings

awakening

salt

tree

lips;

mid

way

eclipse

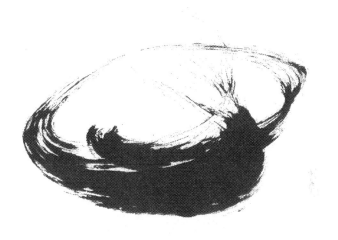

blank

canvas

co-

-mission

complete;

masterpiece

wing

as

brush;

ink

as

dust

angelic

trumpets

ever

sounding;

now,

grounding

every

day

every

hour

in

honor

nonsensical

conundrum;

quantum

leap

t (w) o

one

solar

matter;

well,

inside;

simply,

regalize

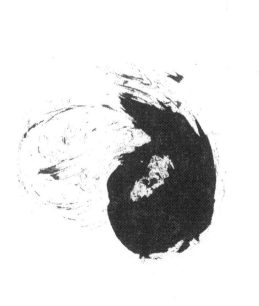

silver

cliff

spires

twist

skyward

wish

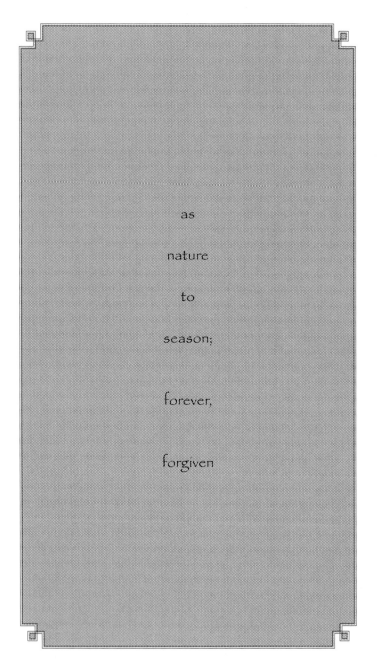

as

nature

to

season;

forever,

forgiven

emissarial

oneness;

its

message;

of

love

seedlings

arise;

surprise

but

not

surprise

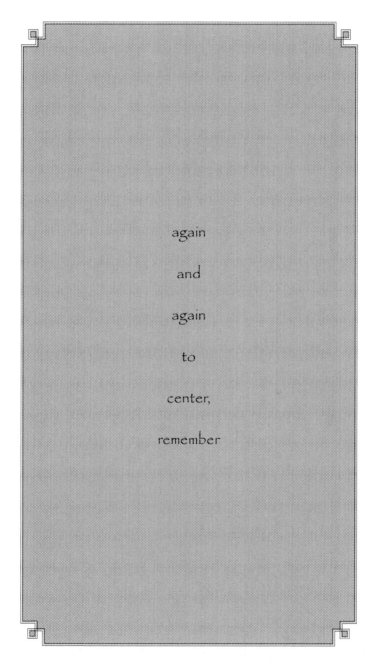

again

and

again

to

center,

remember

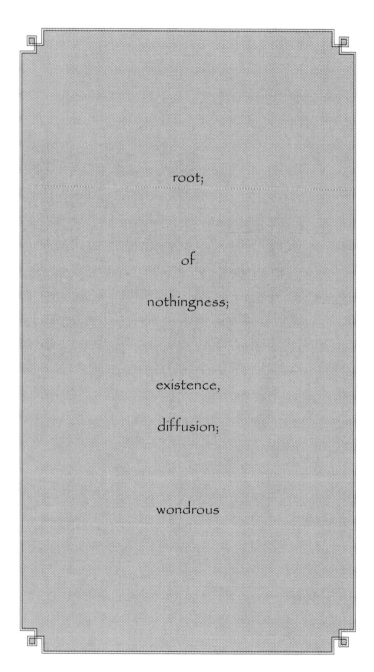

root;

of

nothingness;

existence,

diffusion;

wondrous

rain

box

sky

drops

mind's

cause

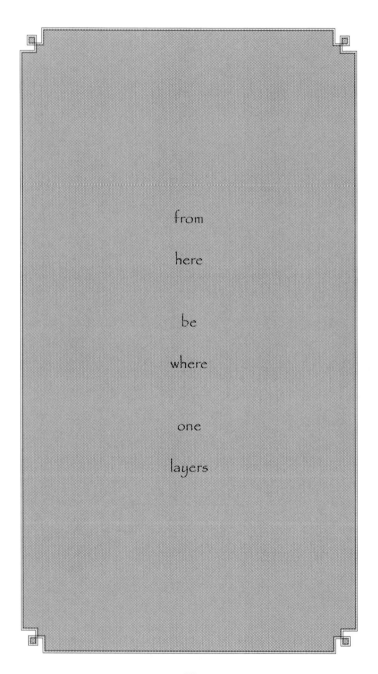

from

here

be

where

one

layers

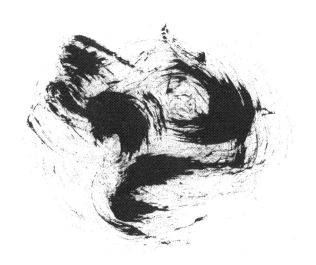

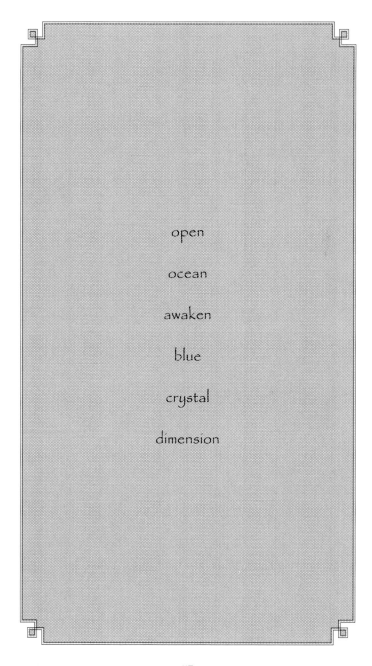

open

ocean

awaken

blue

crystal

dimension

bliss,

is;

all

else

synaptic

static

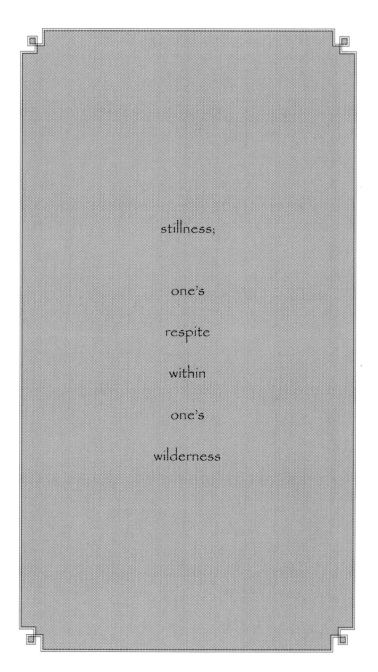

stillness;

one's

respite

within

one's

wilderness

rocky

outcrop

meditation;

internal

eternal

illumination

integration

of

opposites;

yes,

a

prerequisite

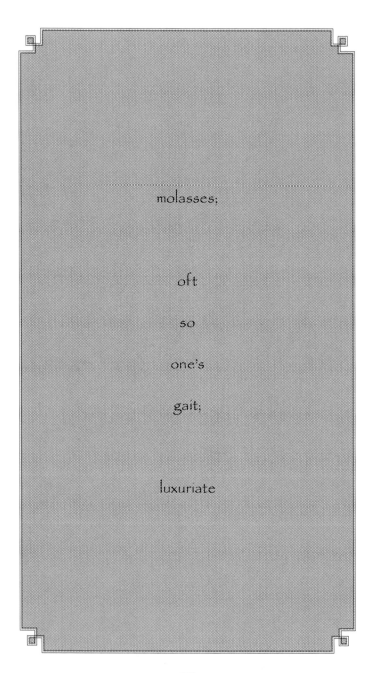

molasses;

oft

so

one's

gait;

luxuriate

almost

forgot;

one

now

one

song

and

perhaps

anew

upon

each

view

center

point's

trip

can't

fathom

it

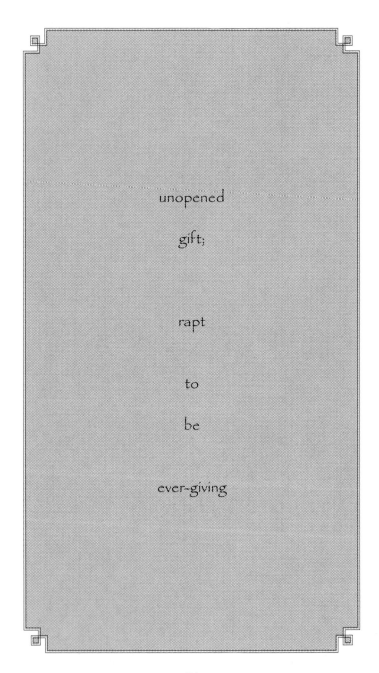

unopened

gift;

rapt

to

be

ever-giving

nothing

knew

what's

true

in

tune

the

volcanic

miraculous;

never

not

active

ever-changing;

life's

simple

arrangement;

illusion's

enchantment

reflect

once;

twice

if

we

bounce

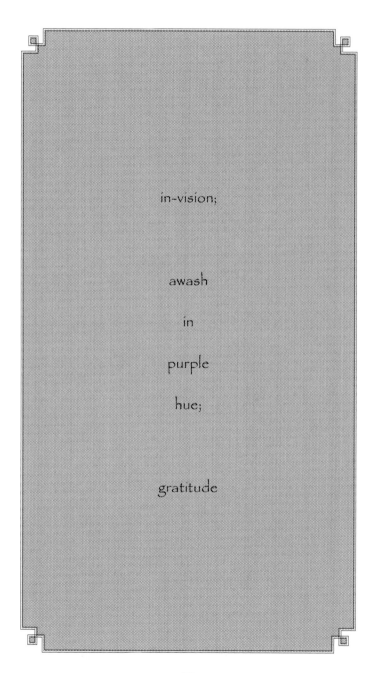

in-vision;

awash

in

purple

hue;

gratitude

lotus;

organic

resonance

of

soul;

inexplicable

non-formulaic;

one's

ingenuity;

in

its

fluidity

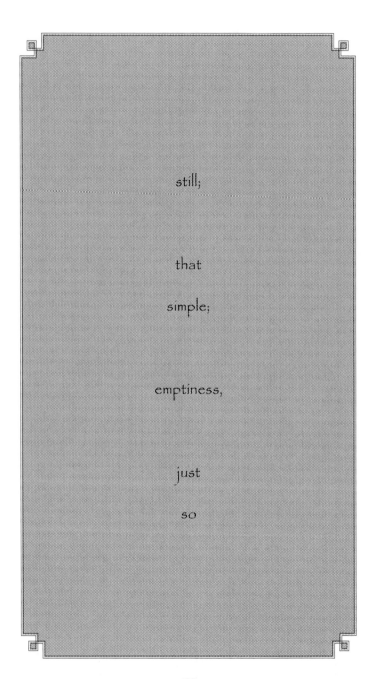

still;

that

simple;

emptiness,

just

so

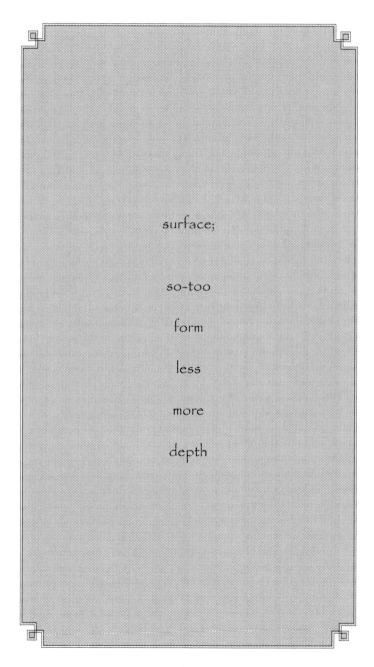

surface;

so-too

form

less

more

depth

snow

drifts;

fire

spits;

nothingness

is

instant

portal;

now

as

was

foretold

one

love

thought

ignites

the

sun

blank

white

page

white

space

erase

worlds

beyond

words

page

pulse

wave